Practical Solutions for Specific Learning Difficulties

Life Skills

by

Jan Poustie

B.Ed. (Dunelm), Cert Ed., RSA Diploma SpLD, AMBDA

A guide to the difficulties in acquiring life skills by those affected by the Specific Learning Difficulties Profile and advice on how to overcome them.

NEXT GENERATION UK 1998

Acknowledgements

Many thanks to:

- Mary Coyle, Steph Smith & Jo Adamson who gave me their time, advice and support
- my family who let me have the peace to write this, provided encouragement AND cooked some of the meals whilst the writing was in progress.

The views expressed by the authoress are her own and do not necessarily represent those who have assisted with the writing of this book.

Mindmap is a trademark of Tony Buzan

Warning

None of the medicines/preparations mentioned in this book should be taken without consultation with one's doctor.

ISBN 1 901544 50 8
2nd edition

A NEXT GENERATION PUBLICATION
First Published in Great Britain in 1998
© Copyright Jan Poustie 1998

Printed By Kampress , Bridgwater, Somerset

Published by Next Generation
17 Medway Close, Taunton, TA1 2NS

CONTENTS

(The text in this book has been set out with an irregular right hand margin to aid those with visual/reading difficulties.)

Chapter 1

The Specific Learning Difficulties Profile

Any of the following conditions can be found in people who have a 'Specific Learning Difficulties Profile'. It is believed by many that these conditions are related to each other primarily through the area of language. Thus individuals affected by the Profile are likely to have a combination of language-based difficulties which can be seen in any, or all, of the areas of written, spoken, heard language plus that of body language. The appropriate use of language, information processing, understanding and acquiring the areas of language can all be affected. Individuals will have a sub set of wide-ranging difficulties (e.g. visual, auditory, memory, perceptual, planning, processing, behavioural and communication difficulties). No two individuals will be alike and many will have more than one condition. Associated with these difficulties are atopic conditions such as hayfever, eczema, asthma and nettle-rash. Travel sickness can also occur and this is associated with the presence of certain aspects of Dyspraxia.

The following conditions are found within the Profile:

Specific Language Impairment (Also known as dysphasia)
A continuum of difficulties experienced by children and young people who have not reached expected competence in communication skills in their first language, and whose teaching and learning is consequently affected. Causes difficulties with expressive language (that which you speak or write) and receptive language (that which you hear/read). Often this group is defined by exclusion: 'They are not autistic, the impairment is not the result of a physical, intellectual or hearing impairment...'(Norma Corkish, AFASIC Chief Executive)

Dyscalculia *Developmental Dyscalculia* - Difficulties in understanding, processing and using numerical/mathematical information that are not caused by another condition within the Specific Learning Difficulty Profile. *Secondary Dyscalculia* - As above but caused by one or more of the other conditions found within the Profile.

Dyslexia (Also called Developmental Dyslexia.) Main difficulties are with the acquisition of spelling and/or reading skills. Can be used as an umbrella term for several of the conditions found within the Specific Learning Difficulties Profile.

Dyspraxia (Also known as Developmental Co-ordination Disorder.) There are various forms of it. All of them relate to difficulties in motor planning and organisation.

Central Auditory Processing Disorder
A dysfunction of the processing of the auditory input causing problems with understanding/processing what is heard.

Attention Deficits (Also known as Attention Deficit Disorder, Attention Deficit Hyperactivity Disorder & Behaviour Inhibition Disorder.) Causes difficulties in concentrating and focusing attention. It affects behaviour and has several forms.

Autistic Spectrum Disorder (Used to be called Autistic Continuum.) Difficulties in social interaction, social communication and in imagination based activities/behaviour.

The following can be found alongside the Profile conditions:

Scotopic Sensitivity Irlen Syndrome
This is a perceptual dysfunction affecting reading and writing based activities as well as depth perception.

Chronic Fatigue Syndrome (CFS) also known as Post Viral Fatigue Syndrome (PVFS) and ME
An illness characterised by fatigue, muscle pain and flu like symptoms occurring after little or no mental/physical effort. It is usually a long term illness which can last for several years. Children (from as young as five years) and adults are affected by it. It causes changes in the brain chemistry which causes the person to develop a secondary form of the Specific Learning Difficulty Profile.

Chapter 2
PERSONAL LIFE

Memory

People affected by memory difficulties can find notepads, lists, Mind Maps and calendars very useful (especially if the person is a visual learner).

Write any entries that you might have to alter in pencil. This avoids crossings-out which can make the person's mind even more confused. The best type of calendar seems to be one with 3-5 columns. Each person can then have a column plus there are spare columns for other items e.g. one column for mum & dad, kids, shopping list and work.

If using Post-its, the person can use different colours for different people. If the individual is affected by glare then the pinks are easier to look at than the yellows. Beware of just putting everything on Post-its and then plastering the walls and kitchen cupboards with them. If that is what is happening the individual needs to organise them by placing different items in different places. Thus all the Post-its relating to the children can go on the front of one kitchen cupboard and all those relating to running the house can go on another.

Losing one's property is a huge problem for many affected by the Profile with perhaps keys, spectacles and handbags/wallets being the items that seem to wander off on their own the most. Solutions to this vary for everyone. A bag worn around the waist is better than a handbag. The keys can go on a hook just inside the door and a particular location e.g. the top of the bookcase can be the home for the spectacles

Planning & organisation

Individuals may have difficulties in deciding priorities and in making decisions. Mindmaps can help in the decision-making process. The items are written on the Mindmap and are then prioritised. It is best if the person limits each decision so that he/she is deciding between two things. Thus if the choice is between playing badminton, walking the dog or reading a book the person can say the following to him/herself:

◊ Which do I prefer badminton or walking the dog?
◊ I prefer walking the dog.
◊ Which do I prefer walking the dog or reading the book?
◊ I prefer reading the book.

On some days the person with this difficulty may not be able to choose even between just two items. If this happens then one way to get the mind out of its difficulty is to:

◊ write each choice on a different piece of paper
◊ close one's eyes and stick a pin/point with a finger at one of the bits of paper.

Sometimes the person will accept the choice of fate and at other times this technique can free the mind to make the decision.

Organising one's day

A Task For The Day Book can be useful for some people as it gives structure to one's day. (These are available at office stationers.)

Organising the paperwork

One of the big problems with Planning & Organisation relates to filing. Everyone may tell the person to file things, put things away etc. but that may be easier said than done. One day the person may place the item in one file and the next day he/she could just as easily file it in another one. Rather than have lots of different files, all with only one bit of paper in them, it can be better to file everything in alphabetical order. This may require an upper case alphabet strip attached to the filing cabinet to aid ease of filing.

9

If there are children in the family a file for each school and one for their doctor's appointments, swimming club etc. can be very useful. It is important to make sure that the files used have closed in sides otherwise if anyone in the family is a little clumsy (as can occur with Dyspraxia) the contents of the file can end up falling into the dog's bowl!

It can help if each member of the family has their own file/box or container of some kind. This can be used for all the papers that seem to come into a house on such a regular basis and the smaller bits and pieces which are left lying around a house. It may take a long time for them to get into the habit of using it. All too often the cry is "I'll do it later." or "I don't need a file because I always put my stuff on the mantelpiece etc." The trouble is, that if several members of the family are affected by the conditions within the SpLD Profile, then everyone may expect to lay everything anywhere and everywhere and still find it there when they want it days or weeks later. If files/boxes do not work then one of the easiest solutions is to dump all the relevant bits of paper, hair bands etc. in a particular place in each person's room. It may not solve the problem entirely but at least it keeps the downstairs part of the house relatively tidy.

Visualisation

Visualisation is the ability to 'see' (imagine) in one's mind what something will look like. This skill is needed to work out what the dress/garden/cake/room etc. will look like when the person has made/decorated it. (We use the same skill when trying to remember a spelling, the layout of a sum or musical notation.)

Some things are easier to visualise than others and just because one has a difficulty in visualising one type of information it does not mean that all visualisation tasks will be affected. The individual may be good at visualising colour but poor at visualising what a meal or a garment will be like when it is made. Once the person realises where their strengths and weaknesses lie he/she can then buy appropriate materials to help achieve a given task. From the point of view of some people the picture on the front of a sewing pattern (if it is a diagram rather than a photo of the made-up garment) may not be of much use. It does not give a good enough guide to the final appearance of the item. However, a cookbook with plenty of photos (which give a real representation of the finished product) may be much more useful and enable the cook to create a lovely meal. Nowadays there is computer software for every occasion and purpose and so if someone with poor visualisation skills wants to plan a garden, decorate a room the software exists to help.

Energy

Regular intake of food
Recently research has shown that certainly in the case of Dyslexia, individuals are working the brain much harder when processing information e.g. reading. This is likely to be true for all of us who are affected by the Specific Learning Difficulty Profile conditions.

More brain activity means that the body uses more energy. Affected individuals who are students (or who are in work) may need a more regular intake of food and drink than their peers. Students can easily run out of energy during the day and eat part of their lunch at break time, so, leaving not enough food for the rest of the day. Such students may be extremely irritable/hyperactive when they leave school and when they arrive home they raid the larder/fridge and crash out on the sofa for an hour. A solution would be a high calorie product which contains mixed carbohydrate and protein e.g. chewy bars/ nutribars or fruit to eat during the morning and afternoon breaks.

Regular intake of drink
Children may go all day at school without a drink and then feel ill at the end of the day because they have become dehydrated. They need to have at least two drinks during the day.

Easy-to-eat foods

Those with Articulatory Dyspraxia will need to have foods that are quick to eat. If this need is not met they can become self-conscious about the time it takes to eat, plus lose out on valuable social time with other children. They also can miss out on opportunities to attend clubs held during the lunch-time at school. They (along with others affected by different forms of Dyspraxia) will need foods that are not messy to eat. They may also need drinks in age-appropriate flasks/bottles etc. that will not easily spill the liquid when knocked over, or, when they are handled poorly.

Those affected by ME will have fluctuating energy levels throughout the day. These fluctuations may not relate to the amount of energy expended on that day and they can also have periods of hyperactivity. They like those with Attention Deficits may have days/periods of reduced appetite.

Spatial skills

Those affected by Dyspraxia and Dyscalculia may have weak spatial skills. Some spatial skills may be intact even though others may be poor. Thus a person can have poor awareness of where their body is in space but may know when a picture is crooked and know to the last millimetre whether a piece of furniture will fit into a particular space. Another aspect of spatial skills is used when manoeuvring a piece of furniture through a doorway - an essential skill for removal men!

Sleep

Sleep difficulties (affecting both children and adults) are associated with Attention Deficits, Autistic Spectrum Disorder and any of the other SpLD Profile conditions due to stress and anxiety. The parents of a child who has difficulty in going to sleep, and staying asleep, can become exhausted. They may get very little respite as the child is unlikely to be invited to stay the weekend with anyone! Keeping the child constantly warm at night can help, though care must be taken to ensure that he/she does not overheat.

Putting the central heating on all night is an expensive solution. A cheaper one would be the use of an electric blanket that is suitable for all night use. (Make sure that it has a variety of settings and do not use one if the child is likely to be unsafe with it e.g. uses scissors on the bed, pours drinks over the plug etc.).

A kitten/puppy to keep the child company at night may help. However, both will need training (which can be a lot of work) and not all cats and dogs like being cuddled. Sometimes a bed-time routine can help e.g. a story followed by a milky drink. It is best not to have a drink which has a lot of chocolate in it at night as that can keep the child awake. For the older person (60+ years) coffee has been found to be effective.

There are various homeopathic preparations for adults that can be bought at health food shops and chemists e.g. Noctura and Peaceful Relaxation. Both adults and children can use Avena Sativa but you may have to go to a registered homeopath to obtain it. Five Flower Remedy (available from Health Food Shops) can make the exhaustion more bearable and help relax the child and parent. (It is also suitable for daytime use.)

Reading a book, or listening to tapes, can help some people get to sleep but some people/children find story tapes/stories so exciting that they stay awake to listen/read to the end. If the worst comes to the worst the parent of a child who cannot go to sleep can read the most boring book that they can find. This may not always work, as what is boring to one person is not boring to another as one mum found out. She had regularly read car repair manuals to her daughter to get her to sleep and the girl grew up to have an interest

in repairing cars! It is important to remember that a child affected by Autistic Spectrum Disorder may thoroughly enjoy listening to lists of car makes, engine sizes etc. so it is a case of reader beware!

Of course, the person could always listen to the radio but again that may prove too exciting - though for a young child just listening to human voices can help. If that is the case, the BBC's World Service and Radio 4 can be of use. Classical music can help some people and this is available on various private stations as well as BBC Radio 3.

For some people (e.g. those affected by Attention Deficits) the problem is not being able to get to sleep because they have so many ideas running through their head. Here, a small tape recorder can be placed by the bed and used to tape the thoughts that are keeping them awake. An alternative solution is to use a small notepad to write down (or Mind Map) one's thoughts.

Sometimes the only solution may be to get up, make a drink, sit at the computer and write down all your ideas and then (if you are lucky and having cleared your mind of thoughts) you might get to sleep. This can also be the solution to restless sleeping through the night and waking up in the early hours of the morning. This sort of sleep disturbance can accompany ME and the stress brought on by having to cope with the conditions within the SpLD Profile or having to live with someone affected by it! Such a sleep pattern can also be part of the conditions themselves e.g. Attention Deficits.

There is always a bright side to life. The benefit of such an early rise can be the morning's dawn chorus and the reading of a good book without the rest of the household disturbing you!

Chapter 3
COMMUNICATION

Using the telephone

Acquiring telephone skills can be a difficulty for those affected by Autistic Spectrum Disorder, Specific Language Impairment, Central Auditory Processing Disorder, Attention Deficits, Dyscalulia and Dyslexia. Using a telephone has become an essential skill. It is easier to acquire this skill if there has been plenty of early experience and the various stages mentioned below are followed at whatever age the tuition in this skill starts. *(For convenience no matter what the age of the student 'child' has been used in the instructions below.)*

Stage 1 -Talking to close family

The parents encourage the child to use the telephone from the moment that he/she can say hello. This may just be to say "Hello" and "Goodbye granny." The child can, instead of writing thank you notes, make a thank you call for Christmas and birthday presents.

Stage 2 -Talking to friends & relatives
The next stage would be for the child to ring relatives and school

friends. The parents need to dial the number (so avoiding problems of sequencing for those affected by Dyslexia and pressing the wrong numbers for those affected by Dyscalculia). Do not expect the child to be able to cope with making the first contact. The parent should do this by holding onto the phone until the person the child wants to talk to has answered it. Some children, especially those with Severe Language Impairment, will have to work out (and then rehearse) a script of what they are going to say with their parent before making the call.

Stage 3- Ringing for information
Continue to rehearse conversations before they are made. The parent now watches (and is there to assist if things go wrong) whilst the child does the dialling. Only once the child is fully confident in ringing friends and relatives should he/she be asked to ring someone that he/she does not know. A good introduction to this sort of call might be to ring the speaking clock (dial 123) where no   response is expected on the part of the caller or Directory Enquiries (dial 192) to obtain a phone number.

Stage 4 - Answering the phone
This has to be thoroughly prepared beforehand and it is best if it is someone that the child knows who makes the first few calls. Prior to taking the call the child rehearses with the parent how he/she will respond to the call by:
1   saying the number e.g. "01 823 289 559"
2   saying "Hello, this is ....(child's name) speaking"
3   Then WAIT for the person to respond
The parent should be present throughout the call. The caller should just speak to the child for a few minutes e.g. asking how they are getting on at school, about their hobbies etc. and then should ask to be passed on to the parent.

Stage 5- Taking a message
This can be a very frightening experience for someone who is not confident in using the phone as he/she can fear that they will mishear, make a fool of themselves etc. Thorough rehearsing of the call beforehand is essential. Initially, it is best if it is someone that the child knows who makes the first few calls and that the parent is in attendance throughout the call to give moral support to the child. The parent puts the child into control by giving him/her a telephone message pad or the specially designed Solutions

16

Telephone Sheet on which to record the relevant information. The latter is in the 'Solutions for overcoming creative & factual writing difficulties' guide (published by Next Generation).

A message pad/Solutions Telephone Sheet and a pen/pencil must be kept by the phone. As soon as the phone rings the child answers it. No matter what the caller says the child always responds by saying:

1. Please hold the line while I fetch some paper and a pen
(This is a lie but it gives the child time to calm and prepare him/ herself ready to take control of the call)

If the caller says don't bother just say "I always like to write messages down and put the phone down for a few seconds.
The child is now in control of the call. He/she picks up the pen and then asks the following questions and writes down the answers on the telephone pad/Solutions telephone sheet.

2. Could you say your name again please?
3. Could you spell that please?
(Nowadays no-one is surprised if you ask them how to spell their name.)

4. Could you tell me your telephone number please?
5. Can I check your number its ....
(Repeat back the number to the caller)

6. Who do you want me to give the message to?
7. What is your message?
8. Could you speak a bit slower please?
(This only needs to be done if the person is speaking too fast)

9. Thanks for calling. I'll give message to ....
(Says the name of the person that the message is for.)

Older students can have a problem with using the technique in Stage 5 as they may well be receiving a call from one of their relation/ friends of the family and both the student and the caller know each other well. Family members will tolerate the student going through the whole process at Stage 5 but one's brothers friends may not be sympathetic to the needs of the student! One solution is to just leave the answer phone on and so never have to cope with the stress of taking the message down wrong (and the brother failing to meet up with his friends at the right time and in the right place). Alternatively, the brother can explain to his friends that they can help the student by making sure that he is able to cope with the task of writing down the message. Thus the friends should not say the information too quickly and should check that the student has got it right without embarrassing him.

The problems that occur when using a phone

Knowing the other person's emotional state

Some people, such as those with Attention Deficits and Specific Language Impairment have difficulties in understanding tonal cues (e.g. pitch and tone of voice) and so cannot interpret the speaker's emotional state just by listening to the voice.

A poor sense of time

Some people e.g. those affected by Attention Deficits, Autistic Spectrum Disorder, Dyspraxia and Dyscalculia) may have a poor sense of time. This means that they may have no idea how long they have been on the phone and

so can run up large phone bills without realising it. A simple solution to this is to use a kitchen timer to time the maximum time for the call. When it goes off they just say goodbye - but that does take a lot of self-control and all too often one can get lost in the conversation again. Fortunately, one can now get telephones that tell one how long the call is - these cost about £30 and are available from High Street shops such as Tandy.

People who have a poor time sense will need to be very careful when using the internet as otherwise they could end up with very expensive phone bills!

Other communication based difficulties

Vision

Our eyes both provide and receive a great deal of information when communicating. Those affected by Autistic Spectrum Disorder may not be able to look at a person's eyes and face and so miss all these body cues.

Other people may be affected by Occulomotor Delay/Dyspraxia, and either of these conditions will cause difficulties in learning to read to write. There is no one solution to these difficulties. For some glasses fitted with 0.1 lenses may help. Others will need eye exercises that help with tasks such as tracking the text from left to right. A useful exercise is for the person to start at the top left hand corner of a window (of a room, car windscreen etc.) and go round the edge of it with their eyes in a clockwise direction. They can hold out a finger in front of them as a guide to make the task easier. Some may find that coloured lenses may help. All groups may find it better if the brightness on the computer screen is reduced and some may find changing the background colour on the screen helps too.

Reading & writing difficulties

Such difficulties may occur as part of Dyslexia, Occulomotor Delay, Occulomotor Dyspraxia, Scotopic Sensitivity Irlen Syndrome and ME. Not many people are aware that Dyslexia can be acquired if a person contracts ME. This condition can affect one's ability to read and spell and calculate. ME can also cause many of the difficulties that we associate with the Specific Learning Difficulty Profile e.g. concentration and co-ordination difficulties. The youngest age for contracting ME so far is five years old. If fatigue and muscle pain are found alongside Dyslexia than ME should be considered. Dyslexia can also be secondary e.g. as a result of another condition within the Profile. Thus, for instance, those affected by Attention Deficits may not focus their concentration long enough to learn to read, spell and write.

Body language

Those affected by Attention Deficits, and Autistic Spectrum Disorder may have difficulties in interpreting body language. Body language includes facial expressions as well as the movements of the various parts of the body. People without difficulties in this area use body language cues to gain a huge amount of information during a conversation. Those with difficulties may have problems in interpreting it and may (along with those affected by Dyspraxia) give out inappropriate body language information themselves. All groups have to be taught how to interpret it and how to use it.

It is absolutely vital that this is done as early as possible. If this is not done before the child starts playgroup or nursery he/she may not react when adults use body language cues and tone of voice to show their displeasure at the child's work/behaviour. In such cases when the person does become annoyed with the child it can seem as though its 'coming like a bolt from the blue'. This can be very distressing to (and confusing for) the child .

The need to draw attention to how the body shows emotions
The solution to this problem is to literally draw the child's attention to the way the face creases and changes as the parent/carer displays one emotion and then another. It is best to do two emotions at a time e.g. from happy to sad. In the same way attention should be drawn to how the whole body looks when different emotions are being shown.

The effects on the marriage

The presence of Specific Learning Difficulties within the family can cause marriages to break down. This happens due to several factors e.g. weak communication skills within the family, the conditions themselves (and the affect they have upon family life) and that commonly each parent views/reacts to the problems differently.

Chapter 4
THE INTIMATE SIDE OF LIFE

Toilet needs

Some conditions affect one's ability to sit on the toilet and wipe one's bottom efficiently e.g. difficulties in staying on task (Attention Deficits) and poor fine motor control, balance and body awareness (Dyspraxia).

Those with Dyspraxia may have difficulties in using internal sanitary protection during a period. Girls may need to be shown several times how to insert the tampon. It is likely that they will have to insert their fingers into the vagina first to get an idea of the correct angle. They may need to be shown several times how to use external sanitary towels as they can be quite fiddly (especially if they are the sort with wings that give greater protection). There may be difficulties in being able to cleanse themselves adequately during a period (and after the birth of a baby). If this is the case use a bidet. The central fountain type of bidet is best but it usually costs more to install. It has the added advantage that it can then be used to wash the baby when tiny!

Those affected by Dyspraxia and/or Autistic Spectrum Disorder may be texturally over/under sensitive so the toilet roll may need to be very soft. A variety which may be suitable is Kleenex Quilted (they also produce a very soft tissue for blowing one's nose called Kleenex Ultra Balm). Parents may have to be careful not to rub too hard when drying the child. They may also have to check that the child does not rub too hard to clean themselves as they can make their skin sore. (Moist toilet tissue wipes such as the Boots or Andrex brands may be used if this is the case.) Hand towels and flannels may be too rough, or soft, for this group.

Under/over sensitivity can continue into adulthood so adults may need to take the same precautions. Indeed, some may need to use a hair dryer instead of a towel to dry themselves.

Bathing

Those affected by Dyspraxia or Autistic Spectrum Disorder may only tolerate baths and may dislike, or positively hate, the feel of water falling on them. Such individuals will dislike having a shower, having their hair washed or being out in the rain.

This can be a problem when camping with a child as most camp sites offer showers rather than baths. When the child is young one can make do with the large sinks available for washing babies that are found in the better class of site. However, once the child becomes too big for  this the solution is either a strip wash using a bowl in the tent or accepting a less than normal standard of hygiene. The other alternative is to camp by the sea and use the sea as a source of washing but beware some children in this group cannot abide sand either!

Hair, nail & dental care

People are gauged by their appearance. If any one of these aspects of personal presentation is poor then the wrong impression can be given. Each of these are important aspects of personal hygiene. They contribute to the way in which other people respond to the individual. Poor skills in this area can affect whether the person looks smart enough for the workplace.

Those with Dyspraxia may have an over/under sensitive scalp, mouth or nails. Such individuals are likely to dislike having their hair and/or nails touched. They may be distressed when their hair is cut, feel uncomfortable when their nails are cut and find teeth cleaning unpleasant.

Some individuals may only have one of these areas affected e.g. may dislike having their hair handled but not be affected by their teeth being cleaned.

Hair:

Difficulties in having a child's hair cut can stem from various conditions e.g. lack of co-operation with the hair dresser (Autistic Spectrum Disorder) not sitting still long enough to have their hair cut (Attention Deficits) and dislike of having their hair touched/cut  (Autistic Spectrum Disorder and Dyspraxia). For all of these groups a hairdresser that comes to your house may be the best solution. If the child likes TV the parent can always have a video on whilst the hairdresser is working. Adults affected by Dyspraxia may not be able to do their daughter's hair in attractive styles e.g. bunches & pony tails.

Dealing with head lice can be a problem - especially if the child makes a big fuss whenever you go near his/her hair or wash it. There is the added complication that the recommended treatment for head lice now involves the head being smothered in conditioner for ten minutes plus a great deal of combing. Some people may choose to use the chemical preparations that are available but (apart from the fact that they are now thought to be fairly ineffective) there is the concern that they have been implicated in individuals contracting ME through using them. Some children may be over sensitive to smell (Dyspraxia, Autistic Spectrum Disorder) and may hate the smell of the conditioner and/or the chemical preparation.

A solution that can work is to use an electric nit comb - these are available from Argos. They have the advantage of needing the hair to be dry in order to be used (so avoiding having to wash it). The humming sound that they make can enable the child affected by hyperacusis (over sensitivity to some sounds) to become tolerant of some high pitched sounds.

23

(Hyperacusis can be present in those affected by Central Auditory Processing Disorder, Dyspraxia and Autistic Spectrum Disorder.) Use of the electric nit comb enables the child to become accustomed to a high pitched sound similar to that of a dentist drill. Trips to the dentist may then be less stressful. This comb may not be suitable for those affected by Autistic Spectrum Disorder as they may either repeatedly imitate the humming sound, or may be uncomfortable with the vibration.

Nails
It is easier to use nail clippers than scissors and one should teach the child to do it for themselves from an early age.

Dental care

If there is a sensitivity to smell (as can be found as part of Dyspraxia & Autistic Spectrum Disorder) then the teeth can be cleaned without toothpaste. Some people do not mind the taste of mouthwashes and so those can be used too. If fine motor control is weak then the gums and/or mouth can be hurt when cleaning the teeth. For this group an electric toothbrush may be the solution. Toothbrushes that have a two minute timer on them can ensure that the teeth are cleaned for the correct amount of time. There is a high pitched (dentist drill like) sound when they are in use which can be unpleasant for those affected by hyperacusis. A person who cannot tolerate an electric nit comb may be quite happy using an electric toothbrush and vice versa.

Clothing & dress sense
Individuals affected by Dyspraxia may lack the fine motor control to put the finishing touches to their clothes e.g. pocket flaps half in half out of the pocket. They may also only be comfortable in loose clothes. Such individuals may need help in choosing suitable work clothes that are not fussy but look smart enough for the workplace. There are various solutions if the repeated 'trying on' which is part of the clothing selection process is stressful for the individual. When taking a person with this difficulty shopping it is best to restrict the number of shops visited to a maximum of three and

 limit the number of garments tried on in each shop to one or two. If making a decision as to which garment is the most suitable is a problem then always limit the choice to two items. It may also be best if the shopping trip is not a family one but just involves the person with the difficulty and one other person to advise them/reduce the stress of the task. Do not expect a very young child with dressing Dyspraxia to cope with such a shopping expedition - one may have to wait until they are a little older e.g. nine or ten years old before they can cope with the experience. It does take time to enable such individuals to adjust to this aspect of life but it will be worth it once you have confident young people able to shop for themselves.

Those with severe dressing Dyspraxia may be unable to cope with trying on clothes because it is so stressful for them. Such individuals will need someone else to buy their clothes for them. Buying by mail order may also be a suitable option for this group. Choosing clothes this way means that they can try the clothes on a few (or even one at a time) in the comfort of their own home. Some may always be reluctant, or even refuse, to go shopping. Others, like some individuals affected by Autistic Spectrum Disorder, may be so indifferent as to how people view them (or be so uncooperative) that they have very little involvement in choosing the clothes that they wear.

Make-up

Those with fine motor control difficulties (such as those caused by Dyspraxia) may find make-up  difficult to put on. They may need some expert advice. The beauty advisors in department stores may be of help. It would be best to discuss the problem during a weekday rather than on a Saturday when such staff are very busy. The British Red Cross train people to put make-up on patients in hospitals and a local group may have a make-up specialist who is interested in showing your daughter how to do it.

Love & sex

The different conditions within the Specific Learning Difficulties Profile can affect the way in which individuals relate to their partners and cause problems with their intimate relationships. Those affected by Attention Deficits may be all or nothing with regard to having sex. Great for their partner when it is all but rough when it is nothing! Anyone affected by the Profile may have low self-esteem which may make it difficult, if not impossible, to form intimate relationships. (Language difficulties can cause problems in establishing relationships too.) Some are at risk of never forming an intimate relationship with anyone. Both these groups of students will need help and support during their teenage (and   possibly adult) years via introductions into appropriate

 social groups so that they can develop the skills necessary for establishing such relationships. Those affected by Dyspraxia may have fine motor difficulties, difficulties in knowing the amount of pressure to apply and not knowing where they have been touched. This can cause problems in love-making and in putting on condoms.

Social & work relationships

If Specific Language Impairment is present it is likely to affect social and work relationships. Language difficulties are always present as part of Autistic Spectrum Disorder and are likely to be present as part of Dyspraxia. There can also be language difficulties present as part of Dyslexia and Dyscalculia.

Social interaction

The presence of Dyspraxia, Autistic Spectrum Disorder, Specific Language Impairment, Attention Deficits, Central Auditory Processing Disorder can cause problems in developing social interaction skills. There can be difficulties in understanding and following conversations. Knowing, understanding and abiding by the rules of conversation and social

interaction can also be a problem. Members of each of these groups can monopolise the conversation. Those affected by Specific Language Impairment may not talk at all because they are so busy accessing the words that they want to use/interpreting what they hear. Those affected by Autistic Spectrum Disorder may elect to be mute. Those affected by Central Auditory Processing Disorder may have both difficulties in processing what they hear and difficulties in listening to the speaker when there is background noise/poor acoustics e.g. swimming pools.

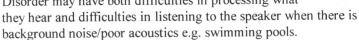

It can help if conversations are rehearsed beforehand. A useful technique (which can be used if the writing/reading skills are better than speech) is for the person to write a play of the conversation. The conversation is then practised with a friend/parent/teacher to build up confidence in the individual. Several plays may have to be written and rehearsed before the individual has the courage to hold the conversation for real.

Parties

Birthday parties can be a very good way of introducing children to the social skills needed for later life. Some children e.g. those affected by Dyspraxia and Attention Deficits may need to be taught how to behave at parties. Such children may need to have a birthday party each year right up to their late teens in order for them to gradually learn appropriate behaviours. When the child is young he/she may elect not to participate in the games. He/she may feel more comfortable helping to run the party e.g. hand out prizes and handle the music for 'pass the parcel' etc.. Some children may become a little too bossy at this stage and may need careful handling during the party to make it a pleasant occasion for

everyone. It may be necessary when they are nine or ten years old to tell them that they must join in at least one of the activities. If affected by Dyspraxia or Attention Deficits the child may fear making a social fool of him/herself whilst those affected by Autistic

27

Spectrum Disorder may be indifferent to other people and/or the way in which other people perceive them. Parties and/or other opportunities for social interaction e.g. going to the cinema with a few friends are a valuable training ground in social skills for the young person. If these opportunities are not provided and encouraged the person can become very isolated in adulthood.

Pubs & night-clubs

Visiting these places can be a very stressful experience for some of those affected by the Specific Learning Difficulty Profile. An over sensitivity to smell (that can be present as part of Dyspraxia and Autistic Spectrum Disorder) can make inhaling other people's smoke a very unpleasant experience. There can be a lot of background noise, music and conversation going on at both venues which can make life difficult for those affected by auditory

 processing difficulties e.g. Central Auditory Processing Disorder, Specific Language Impairment and Attention Deficits. Those affected by Dyspraxia may lack the co-ordination needed to be able to dance well - and therefore may never attempt the task.

Eating & drinking

Those with Dyspraxia may be messy eaters and/or may find it impossible to handle a cocktail party situation where they are holding a drink, a plate and eating at the same time. Such people will find it much easier to sit at a table. Sometimes there is a complete lack of tables at such occasions. In this case the person may be better off just standing by the table and taking the odd sausage roll and eating it without using a plate. Finding a spare chair and eating the food off a plate on one's lap may work for some but not all. At a formal sit down meal it can be embarrassing when there is a messy table when you have finished your meal. Those with Articulatory Dyspraxia may be slow eaters. This group will need easy-to-eat food at lunchtime at school or else they will miss out on social interaction with peers/attendance at lunchtime

clubs. Care will need to be taken to avoid foods that take a lot of chewing e.g. apples.

Those with Autistic Spectrum Disorder, Dyspraxia & Attention Deficits may all be fussy eaters but for different reasons. They may all eat a fairly restricted diet and may only eat certain brands of food, or only eat a diet consisting of just a handful of items which they eat repeatedly. Such individuals may also not be able to cope with foods of mixed consistency e.g. yo-ghurt/soups with bits in them. A mixed diet is essential to remain healthy and so ways need to be found to add some of the foods that the person dislikes into the diet. The cook can mince up items finely and add them to items such as spaghetti bolognaise and soup (this works especially well for young children). Fruit and vegetables can be added to the diet in unusual ways e.g. by adding them to cakes such as Apple Cake and Carrot cake.

If there are concerns about just how restricted the diet is then it can be supplemented by taking multivitamin preparations. Those with Articulatory Dyspraxia may need to take such preparations in a liquid form well into their teens (and possibly into adulthood) because of difficulties in swallowing tablets. Others may accept chewable forms of tablets.

This same difficulty in swallowing tablets applies to those prescribed by a doctor. Some doctors are not very understanding of a person's difficulty in swallow-ing tablets and will automatically prescribe them.

Capsules can be easier to take than round tablets. As long as the tablet does not taste vile (or cannot be taken with food) it can be put into a pleasant piece of food and eaten. The person can also try putting a capsule shaped tablet far back on the tongue (but not far enough back to cause a 'gag reflex') and drink a large drink as though the tablet is not there. A way of introducing the child to swallowing tablets is to get them to swallow the little tiny cooking chocolate buttons that can be bought in shops such as Sainsburys. As they are tiny and taste nice it does not matter if they do not get swallowed as they will not leave an unpleasant taste in the mouth. (Any sharp point of chocolate on the button should be removed before trying to swallow it.). *Do not use the normal sized chocolate buttons for this activity is they could cause the person to choke.*

Some individuals may not drink and eat enough during the day and this can especially apply to school children. This does need

 monitoring otherwise the student can very irritable and difficult to deal with from the moment he/she leaves school until some hours later. (See Chapter 2 - energy section.) The need for easy-to-eat food during the school day may make the diet during school hours less balanced than when he/she is at home. This will not matter as long as the other meals in the day make up for any imbalance in the diet.

An extra drink should be added so that the student does not become dehydrated and they should be greeted by their parent/carer at the end of the school day with food and drink to consume on the way home. Some children may be quite difficult to feed adequately at school such as some of those affected by Attention Deficits. This group (like those with Autistic Spectrum Disorder) may not recognise their own body's signs of hunger. Some of this group do not appear to have consistent levels of appetite (this can occur with ME too) thus they may eat a lot for a few days and then eat very little for a day or so.

Chapter 5

MEASURING

Volume

This is needed for a variety of tasks e.g. cooking, DIY and pouring

out a glass of beer! People with difficulties in this area may try to overfill a glass, jug etc. They may need practise in pouring from a measuring jug into containers of different shapes and then back again in order to gain a concept of volume.

Spatial

Spatial skills are needed for various tasks e.g. knowing whether something will fit into the space that is left, knowing whether the amount of cake mixture on the spoon will fit into the baking case.

Encouraging and enabling children to cook from as young an age as possible will help develop this skill as can playing games like Connect 4.
(A booklet is available from Next Generation on how to play Connect 4 to achieve this affect.)

Length

Some estate agents still use imperial measurements in their house descriptions, others use both metric and imperial.

Some individuals can be confused by the spare bit at the beginning of the rule/ruler. In DIY versions this bit is where the metal ruler is connected to the part that you pull on. In other types of measure this spare section is where a little bit has been added before the 0 to allow for damage to the end of the tape measure. Further confusion can arise when using some extending metal DIY rules where

This tape measure has a spare bit at the beginning to allow for 'wear and tear'.

one is required to include in one's
 measurement the flat section
beneath the box which holds the
extending ruler.

*This flat section at the
bottom of the ruler has to
be included in the
measurement.*

*An analogue
clock
(Digital clocks
just have a
rectangular
space on them
where the
numbers are
displayed.)*

Analogue/digital

Those people who confuse the numeral 5 for the
numeral 2 may find analogue clocks/watches and
scales easier to use but only if the necessary spatial,
language and fractions skills have been acquired.

The vocabulary of time (and an understanding of
what time is) are both necessary in order to tell the
time. Those with Specific Language Impairment may
find learning to tell the time very difficult because
they lack the necessary language. In such cases the
vocabulary (e.g. all the different terms used for the
hands - big/hour hand, little/minute hand and what a
minute, an hour is etc.) should be taught first. Some
people do not understand the concept of time and the sequence of
the day etc. and this too must be taught before any attempt is made
to teach the person how to read the time. *(Next Generation will be
publishing materials to teach these aspects of language in 1999.)*

Scales

Those affected by a form of Dyspraxia which affects fine motor
control may have difficulties in measuring the ingredients for cakes
onto a set of scales. When it comes to measuring heavy objects
there may be difficulties in knowing the units of measurement used
as such scales may not be used very frequently. If scales show both
metric and imperial units there may be confusion as to which units
to use. Analogue scales can be difficult to read at the best of times

32

as some of the little lines marking the ounces and grams are very close together. This task can be impossible for those with visual and/or visual perceptual difficulties e.g. Occulomotor Delay, Occulomotor Dyspraxia or Scotopic Sensitivity Irlen Syndrome).
People affected by any of these conditions may find that the lines blur together and overlap one another.

Sense of time & a need for structure

This can be a problem for both those affected by Attention Deficits, Dyspraxia, Dyscalculia and Autistic Spectrum Disorder and for those who work/live with them! People with poor time awareness may become lost in tasks and/or have no idea how long it will take them to achieve it. They can end up running out of time. They may plan to do a task over a weekend and then find that it takes several weekends to achieve. This can be frustrating for the person affected by the Specific Learning Difficulty Profile and for the rest of the family/work colleagues too. On the other hand those with Autistic Spectrum Disorder may be ruled by time with activities having to be done at certain times of the day etc. Often those affected by Attention Deficits behave much better when their day has a strong structure. In such cases (and in the case of those with Autistic Spectrum Disorder) holidays can be a disaster because the person's routine has changed.

This need for structure can also occur as a result of stress caused by coping with the severe to moderate forms of the conditions within the Profile. This stress reaction can occur in any, or all, of the following: school, college, workplace, home and social life. (*For more details on this area see 'Solutions for overcoming Literacy Difficulties' published by Next Generation.*)

Chapter 6
Budgeting, shopping & DIY Budgeting

Those affected by Dyscalculia may avoid planning and checking accounts whilst those affected by Attention Deficits may find it difficult to be interested in these minor details of life. From a young age children affected by these difficulties should be encouraged to keep a record of their money and help the parents work out the household accounts. Nowadays there are a variety of computer software programs available that can help with keeping such a record - "Quicken" is meant to be one of the better and easy-to-use ones. Beware of very cheap programs (under £20). Some of these may not have enough features to make the task easy e.g. the information may be difficult to save and there may be a very limited layout of the pages.

Saving

The impulsivity of those affected by Attention Deficits (or the daydreamer approach to life that some may have) can result in little interest in saving money. However, if they focus their attention on money matters they can be very efficient at managing money. As with all things the sooner they start the better.

Shopping

Those affected by Dyscalculia may avoid checking change. Those affected by Attention Deficits may easily lose focus without a shopping list, may have a tendency to impulse buy and not be bothered with checking change. They have to be especially careful that they do not build up a large credit card bill. Ei-  ther of these groups may avoid checking accounts. Those affected by Dyspraxia (and ME) may have difficulties in carrying the load.

DIY

This area of life skills can be especially difficult for those affected by the different forms of Dyspraxia because of poor co-ordination in fine motor skills (hand, finger, eye movements) and gross skills (whole body, limbs). Keeping one's balance and applying the correct amount of pressure can also be a problem. Large projects can be a particular difficulty for those affected by Attention Deficits may start the project but not finish it!!! Alternatively, they may spend forever planning it and never get around to doing it!

Painting

Those affected by Dyspraxia or Attention Deficits may find that
 paint pads are much easier to use than brushes. They create much less mess and (unless you overload them) do not drop any paint where you do not want it. A paint coverall is also a must plus having a damp rag available at all times to wipe up drops immediately

Sewing

Nowadays, there are iron-on materials which can be used to hem clothes and repair tears. It is best to use a threader when threading needles. Those affected by Dyspraxia may have difficulties in fine motor control. Despite such problems some may prefer to hand sew rather than use a sewing machine. The person has to remember quite a complicated sequence to thread a sewing machine and this can be a problem for those affected by Dyslexia. (Being able to physically do the sequence of movements needed can be a problem for those affected by Dyspraxia.) Those affected by Attention Deficits may not see the consequence of their actions and so act impulsively. This may result in a very poorly made garment and possible injury to them-selves. Of course if the Attention Deficit person becomes really in-terested in an aspect of sewing they can decide to focus on this skill and can then produce excellent work. (However, the somewhat boring tasks of darning and mending are not likely to interest them!)

Gardening

Some people may have difficulties in classifying (e.g. those affected by Dyspraxia or Dyscalculia) and so will pull up the plants along with the weeds! For this group it is best to plant bushes or

spend a lot of time grabbing the flowers from the
rubbish heap! Those affected by Dyspraxia may need to be
shown how to use the tools effectively. The presence of
Dyslexia may cause individuals to have difficulties in
reading the instructions on bottles of weedkillers etc.

Car maintenance

There may be difficulties in following the instructions/diagrams in
the car manual. These can arise from a variety of conditions e.g.
reading text (Dyslexia) reading diagrams (Dyspraxia/ Dyscalculia).
Difficulties in following the diagrams may be due to problems in
relating what the person sees in the manual to what they see (at
possibly a different angle) on the car. Poor fine motor control
difficulties will result in problems in controlling tools. A person may
have poor writing skills alongside good mechanical skills.

Accidents

Various aspects of the SpLD Profile conditions may increase the
likelihood of an accident. The impulsive behaviour which can be
seen as part of Attention Deficits can lead the person to act without
thinking of the consequences. The lack of awareness of danger
(found in Attention Deficits and Autistic Spectrum Disorder) can
also result in injury or damage. People affected by these conditions
may ignore, not read or obey labels/safety precautions and instructions unless closely monitored by others. The temper tantrum that
then occurs can further damage the item! Dyspraxia may cause the
person to use too much pressure on an item or damage it because of
poor fine motor control difficulties making tools difficult to use/
control. This can also result in damage to spectacles. (Spring loaded
or plastic ones seem to be the most hardwearing.) Women are more
likely to have an accident before a period! Those affected by both
Dyspraxia & Attention Deficits may 'fight' with packaging. They
may (especially if they are in a hurry) use an inappropriate tool to
open it thus putting them at risk of having an accident e.g. removing
the cellophane from a video cassette with a carving knife because
they want to video a programme NOW!

Chapter 7

COOKING

Different aspects of cooking can be a problem for those affected by Dyspraxia, Dyscalculia, Autistic Spectrum Disorder and Dyslexia. The latter occurs when reading cookery books etc. and remembering the correct sequence e.g. using a timer.

The tools

Different implements are used for various preparation tasks e.g. chopping, peeling etc.. There are a wide variety of types of each tool and it is essential that those with co-ordination difficulties are given a selection of tools and shown how each one should be used. The individual can then choose to use the one that he/she finds the easiest to control. Blunt tools take more effort to use than sharp ones but children should always be supervised when using tools.

The cooker

There are several different types of cooker. If co-ordination/concentration difficulties are present then a microwave is one of the safest and easiest to use as there is less risk of the operator being burnt. The individual will have to be aware that liquids can have a volcanic eruption in them if they are not stirred and that the cooking containers can become very hot. One of the advantages of using the microwave for the schoolchild is that the cooking itself will not take long and so they will have more time during the lesson to wash up etc. A disadvantage may be that the child will forget that they cannot put anything made out of metal in it and leave a spoon etc. in a mix that they are cooking.

 ### The hob

Once the individual has gained confidence with the microwave then he/she can progress to using the hob e.g. boiling potatoes, stews etc.. Do not introduce frying at this point unless making something with very little oil as the spitting can be quite frightening. Frying can also be dangerous. The consequences of the easily distracted Attention Deficit child wandering off and leaving it are too terrible to contemplate! The person who is unaware of danger may not realise when they accidentally drop something into hot oil (or any other hot liquid) that they cannot put their hand into the container to retrieve it!

Using the oven
The next stage is using the oven. Oven doors which open downwards are likely to be the most dangerous as one has to reach over the door to get to the food. Such doors also throw all the heat upwards to where your hand is opening the door. Therefore, if possible use a side door oven. A pair of oven gloves which has a piece of material joining the two gloves is safer than just one glove when taking food out or putting it into the oven.

A barbecue can be quite dangerous for many of those affected by the Specific Learning Difficulty Profile. The easily distracted and impulsive (or day-dreaming) person with Attention Deficits is liable to end up with burnt food. Mind, where Attention Deficits is concerned that can happen with virtually any method of cooking! The person with co-ordination difficulties may find it very fiddly to turn the food over using the usual barbecue tools. The young child affected by either Attention Deficits or Autistic Spectrum Disorder may have so little awareness of danger that he/she is burnt by the barbecue and/or causes danger to others..

It is best to start cooking techniques with vegetables and cakes as the former will develop control of the cooking tools and the latter taste nice! Those affected by Dyspraxia/Autistic Spectrum Disorder may have great sensitivity regarding the smell of meat, fish etc. and touching the actual cooking mixture e.g. dough, cake mix. The person with Autistic Spectrum Disorder may only get as far as watching the food processor blades go round and round and round ....!   .

Although it may be common to teach children as young as nine years to make a cup of tea it may be best to delay teaching this skill

38

until ten or even eleven years if severe co-ordination difficulties/Attention Deficits are present. If the child is affected by Autistic Spectrum Disorder remember that whatever you do the first time when you show them how to make tea you are likely to have to do for evermore! (This is an extremely wearing aspect of  this condition.) If there are concerns about the child supporting the weight of the kettle when making the tea it might be safer for him/ her to make tea by heating a mug of water in the microwave and adding a teabag. Again, one does have to be careful not to fill the mug too high -after all half a cup of tea is better than none! This quantity will allow enough room to stir the water whilst the mug is still in the microwave to prevent the volcano effect.

Timers
The use of kitchen timers can ensure that the meal is either cooked
 enough or not burnt. There are various types available and all of them require that the cook calculates how long the food will need to be in the oven, or, in the case of some oven timers the time when the food will be ready. Those affected by Dyscalculia can be at a distinct disadvantage here. It can be very frustrating to go to the effort of making the meal only to ruin it because of a failure in working out the time. The distractibility of Attention Deficits can be just as bad because one can forget to set the oven correctly so that there is no nice roast dinner in the oven on your return - extremely frustrating on a cold winter's day!

The main types of timer are:
♦ Little kitchen timers. The easiest ones to use and they have the advantage of being portable. (Though that can be a disadvantage if the person mislays things on a regular basis.) Make sure that there is a line for each minute all the way round - some only mark every five minutes.
♦ Digital ones may be more suitable for some people than analogue ones e.g. if there is visual/perceptual confusion between the 5 and the 2.

♦   The timers on cookers can be fiddly to use.

Cooker controls

Some cookers require three knobs to be turned before the oven will come on - forgetting to switch one on will result in no meal! Some gas hob controls require spatial skills as they just have symbols for a small flame, a medium flame and a big flame. They may need the control to be turned all  the way round to the big flame to ignite and then be turned down. This can cause problems for those with Attention Deficits as they may become distracted and so forget to turn it down- that usually results in burnt saucepans and food!. The same result can occur through spatial difficulties where the person does not judge the distance correctly and so does not turn it down enough (or up enough) for the correct cooking temperature. Those with co-ordination difficulties can find some cooker knobs too stiff to turn with any ease.

Some people may have difficulties in interpreting the mini hob diagrams on the cooker which tell the cook which knob applies to which hob plate. Sometimes gas rings have to be lit by hand e.g. if the cooker's electronic lighter is faulty (or if the gas ring is dirty. If in such cases the cook misreads the hob diagram and switches the wrong ring on there can be a dangerous escape of gas into the kitchen. If the cook is using an electric cooker then the wrong electric hob may be switched on which can result in the cook (or another person) burning themselves on it.

Opening containers

If affected by Dyspraxia it may be impossible to use a tin opener or a nutcracker which requires the use of a lot of pressure. WL Housewares makes an easy to use tin opener. The person slides its two arms (one on top of the other) to pierce the can and then turns the easy-to-hold key to open it. Gadgets are also available to make it easier to open jars.

Chapter 8
CHILDCARE

All the conditions within the Specific Learning Difficulties Profile can cause problems with this area of life. They can be present in the child and/or the parents.

Stress

Having children, and bringing them up, is extremely demanding. Some of those affected by the Profile may find it difficult enough to cope with their own difficulties for normal day-to-day life without the extra demands of childcare! Comments by relatives/friends who know nothing of the SpLD conditions (and how they affect the child) only make this situation worse. Often the parents (especially the mum) are on the receiving end of verbal attacks/criticism regarding the behaviour of the child and how they are 'spoiling him' with regard to getting him to settle at night, eat properly etc.. Sometimes one set of 'in-laws' treat the situation with compassion and the others treat it with negative criticism. This can drive a wedge between the parents, as can the situation when one parent realises that the child has difficulties whilst the other does not. All of this stress can result in the marriage/relationship being under severe strain with the situation worsening once learning difficulties become apparent at school. Attending Relate (or reading some of their books) and talking to one's local support group can be very helpful. (See Chapter 14 for further details.)

Changing nappies

Those affected by Dyspraxia may have considerable difficulties in co-ordinating their own movements without coping with a wriggler -who does not like having his/her nappy changed. It is certainly unlikely that the parent will be able to change the baby on her lap. It is much easier for such parents if two nappy changing areas are installed - one upstairs and one downstairs. The strain of giving birth can be very great for the mum affected by Dyspraxia and she may well need to make her life as easy as possible after the birth.

Having two nappy changing areas means less walking up and down stairs. It also reduces the amount of carrying of the baby that needs to be done. Disposable nappies are likely to be easier to use than terry ones and if fine motor control is not good they are likely to be safer - no safety pins to worry about. However, there is likely to be some wastage due to getting baby cream on one's fingers, pulling the sticky tabs off by accident etc. etc..

The needs of the child

Those affected by Autistic Spectrum Disorder, Attention Deficits may find it difficult to put the baby's needs first. This can be a real problem for a mother who has a an older child affected by one of these conditions plus a young baby. Adults affected by these conditions may also have difficulties in putting the child's needs first and interpreting the body language of the child

Giving birth

Those affected by Dyspraxia may well have problems in planning and organising the movements of the muscles of the womb and so the second stage of labour may be lengthy. Attending an obstetrician who is also a homeopath can be useful as there are some homeopathic preparations that can improve the strength of the contractions and speed up the labour. The authoress was given Blue Cohosh for her second delivery which was a wonderful four hour delivery compared with the twenty-two hour/forceps assisted ordeal of the first one. The first birth may be the hardest simply be- cause the mum has not had to plan and organise this set of muscles before.

Feeding - (baby)

Babies affected by Articulatory Dyspraxia are likely to have feeding problems. They may take a long time to feed, need lots of feeds, have problems with latching on/ releasing from the nipple. If the baby takes a long time to feed then preparations such as Kamillosan can reduce the tenderness of the breast. Nipple shields can both reduce the discomfort of long periods of breastfeeding and provide the baby with something larger to latch on to. Babies with

42

a sensitivity to the smell of their mother's perspiration (Dyspraxia and Autistic Spectrum Disorder) may fight the breast.

Bottle feeding the baby may also not be easy. The presence of Dyslexia may cause difficulties in reading the milk preparation instructions and leaflets regarding the baby's health. Numbers can be confused (Dyslexia) and misread (Dyslexia, Dyspraxia, Occulomotor Dyspraxia). Too much pressure could be used when putting the milk into the scoop (Dyspraxia) resulting in too rich a feed. Teat sizes and shapes may need to be experimented with if the baby has Articulatory Dyspraxia. The baby may be transferred to a Soya milk if lactose intolerance is thought to be present but some of our children can be allergic to soya! The local group of the National Childbirth Trust can provide advice on breastfeeding as can the family's health visitor.

Feeding - (young child)
Feeding difficulties can affect those with Attention Deficits, Dyspraxia and Autistic Spectrum Disorder. Such individuals may be very fussy about what they eat due to textural/oral/smell sensitivity. Some do not appear to recognise when they are thirsty and/or hungry and so eat and drink too little. Those affected by Autistic Spectrum Disorder may drink until they vomit. All groups may give themselves a very restricted diet which is difficult to change (A multivitamin supplement is always wise in such cases but beware of buying the types with colours in them as this can cause eczema and/or behavioural problems, in some children.) Constipation may result from a restricted diet. Parents/ mothers-in-law etc. can be very critical/challenging of the diet and this can create a lot of stress within the family. It is important to remember that a meal is adequate as long as it contains protein, carbohydrate and either a vegetable OR a fruit A banana with grated cheese and a drink of milk is an odd meal but it will feed the child!

Child rearing
The presence of a condition which has a behavioural element (e.g. Attention Deficits, Dyspraxia and Autistic Spectrum Disorder) can

cause great problems within the family. One family member affected by these conditions is stressful on all the other family members and those families with more than one person affected are likely to find it very hard going at times. (Attention Deficits in both the child and a parent makes a particularly volatile mix - both have difficulties in controlling emotions and their reactions to the emotions of the other.)

Ground rules for survival may have to be established. Roping in relatives to give the parents some respite from childcare is also advisable but unfortunately, in today's society that is not always possible as often young families are living far away from siblings and grandparents. If the parents are in the position where they have very little respite from the child they should do everything possible to improve their quality of life. Giving each other short breaks out of the house can be helpful - even an hour away from a very demanding child is better than nothing.

If the family cannot afford baby sitters then renting videos can bring some relaxation into the house. (Humorous ones are the best type to watch as laughing has been shown to reduce stress.) Babysitting circles can be a free source of babysitting but have the disadvantage that the parent is expected to baby sit someone else's child in return. Such circles are unlikely to be an option for most parents of children with Attention Deficits and Autistic Spectrum Disorder for two reasons. Firstly, the parents may well be too exhausted to baby sit anyone else's child. Secondly, it is usually expected that the child is asleep (or at least in bed) when the baby-sitter arrives and this may rarely be the case with such children.

Homeopathic medicine, prescribed by a registered homeopath, can benefit these children and reduce stress on both child and family. Some homeopaths run specialised children's clinics which are cheaper to attend than a normal consultation. It should be noted that the prescription of such medicines alters according to how the whole person is feeling/behaving/reacting etc. and therefore over- the-counter homeopathic preparations are not likely to be so effective.

Chapter 9

TRAVEL

Road safety

Those affected by Attention Deficits and
Autistic Spectrum Disorder may be lethal to
themselves and others as they may not focus
their attention on the task at hand. The play park over the road
may be far more interesting than holding onto dad's hand as the
lorries hurtle past! Those affected by Dyspraxia may have
difficulties in gauging distances, trajectories and the speed of
moving objects. Children in any of these groups should not be
expected to cross roads safely by themselves until much later than
is usual.

Dynamic perception and/or spatial difficulties

If these difficulties (which are associated with Dyspraxia) are
present it will take longer to learn to cross the road safely e.g. 12+
years instead of the more usual ROSPA figure of 9 years. Thus the
child may need to be ferried to school at the beginning of his/her
attendance at secondary school. This ferrying is most important as
most accidents to children occur in their first year of secondary
school). For toddlers carers may need to use a safety strap which
attaches to the child's wrist. However, in children with a tendency
to eczema the constant rubbing of the wrist may cause eczema to
develop where the strap is in contact with skin. (Children with
Oppositional Defiant Disorder (which can occur alongside
Attention Deficits) may resent the carer trying to control them in
this way which can make every trip to the shops etc. an ordeal.

Cycling

Those affected by Dyspraxia may have difficulties in controlling
the bicycle because of balance and movement problems. Such
children may need stabilisers for much longer or even just one
stabiliser for a while. They may also find it particularly hard to
learn to ride a tricycle because of the angle at which they have to
push the foot when the pedals are attached to the front wheel.

Learning to ride a bike is a good preparation for learning to drive as it gives the rider experience of travelling on the road and following the various road signs and markings. If steering the bike is a problem try marking out white chalk lines on the patio and asking the cyclist to ride the bike along the lines. He/she then has something to aim the bike along.

Gears

Gears that are positioned on (or below) the crossbar are not a good idea for those with balancing difficulties as they can lose balance when reaching down to change gear. It is best if the gears are placed on the handlebars quite close to the handgrip and then only a little movement is necessary to reach them.

Seat position

Normally, it is recommended that the seat is the correct height if one's toes only just touch the ground when standing astride the bike. This is not the case for those with Dyspraxia. They need to feel safe and secure and so will need the seat positioned so that their feet are firmly on the ground. Turning right is always a dangerous manoeuvre when riding a bike and it is most probably not advisable for this group to do so until they have gained plenty of riding experience. Some cyclists feel safer when they can see the vehicles which are about to overtake them via cycling mirrors which are attached to the handlebars.

Handlebar position

Racing bikes do not give a feeling of security to some of those affected by difficulties in maintaining balance as can be found as part of Dyspraxia. This group may much prefer the old fashioned straight handlebars and riding in the traditional 'sit up and beg' position. Once they have gained plenty of experience they may be happy moving on to a racing bike but they are likely to need support and encouragement by their parents during the transition from one type of bike to another

Foot position

People with co-ordination difficulties can feel quite unsafe if their foot is in a foot grip attached to the pedals as they fear that they may not be able to get their foot out of it quickly in an emergency. Some of those affected by Dyspraxia will ride a bike by pushing with their instep, instead of with the sole/ball of the foot. They will need to be shown how to push correctly. Pushing with the instep is not such an efficient movement and it will take more energy to ride the bike.

Driving

At the moment it appears that only a minority of those affected by Dyspraxia learn to drive e.g. those with relatively mild co-ordination difficulties. Although some members of this group can learn to drive a car with normal gears they will find it much easier to learn on an automatic car. This means that they will have both less controls to manipulate and driving will involve fewer co-ordination tasks. As they are likely to have to put more energy into concentrating on the motor tasks of driving they may well tire easily. This group is therefore likely to need frequent breaks during journeys for both food and rest.

Those with Dyspraxia may have difficulties in adjusting to the new layout of controls when changing from one car to another. The person with Autistic Spectrum Disorder may become distressed when the make/model of car is changed, when people sit in different seats from normal and when a different route is taken. Certain 'extras' are very useful to drivers who are affected by Dyspraxia e.g. electric windows/mirrors as they are easier to manoeuvre than manual ones

Of course, those affected by Attention Deficits must learn not to become distracted whilst driving!

Learning to drive

Those affected by Dyspraxia are likely to take longer than normal to learn to drive. The presence of Dyslexia may cause difficulties in remembering the sequence needed to drive the car safely e.g. the sequence of tasks needed to start the car and move it away from the kerb. As many road signs are basically symbols they may also have difficulty in remembering what they mean and in reading the words on the signs.

Those affected by Dyspraxia may find it very difficult to reverse parallel to the kerb. Some people cannot do this walking so no wonder they have difficulties with a car! If this difficulty exists the learner driver should try to do the task by reverse walking round furniture first. Once this is achieved then he/she can go on to use something with wheels e.g. reversing whilst sitting on a typists chair then do the same with a bike. Ideally the learner should have been riding a bike for many years before trying to learn to drive. However, as those affected by Dyspraxia do not always transfer skills easily from one situation to another such individuals may still find it quite hard to learn to drive. For anyone who has difficulties in learning to drive a few lessons in a car simulator would be useful but unfortunately these are not yet widely available.

Reading a map

A wide range of difficulties that can be found as part of the Profile can cause problems in reading and following any type of map. This includes problems with reading the London Underground map and the charts in the stations themselves. Any or all of the following may be present:

◊   Left/right/directional confusion (Dyslexia, Dyspraxia)
◊   Compass difficulties & not being able to follow the route without turning the map round to face the direction in which you are travelling (Dyscalculia/Dyspraxia)
◊   Ignoring the finer details (Attention Deficits)
◊   Not understanding the symbols (Dyslexia/Dyscalculia).
◊   Using an incorrect sequence when reading co-ordinates (Dyslexia/Attention Deficits/Dyscalculia). The co-ordinates are the numbers/letters which define the position of each square on the map)
◊   Meanings of words (Specific Language Impairment)

◊   Reading the words (Dyslexia/Occulomotor Dyspraxia))
◊   Numbers (Dyscalculia) Letter/numbers confusion e.g. 5/2
       (Dyslexia/Occulomotor Dyspraxia)
◊   Spatial relationships difficulties (Dyspraxia)
Any of the above difficulties can also cause the student to have
difficulties in constructing maps at school/college etc.

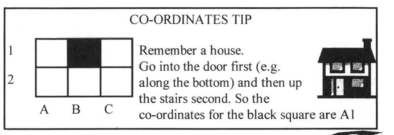

CO-ORDINATES TIP

Remember a house. Go into the door first (e.g. along the bottom) and then up the stairs second. So the co-ordinates for the black square are A1

Train travel

Changing trains (which usually involves changing platforms) can be a problem and may make it necessary to choose a different route across the country which involves fewer, or no, changes. Those affected by Dyslexia may have difficulties in reading the signs especially if they only have a few minutes in which to change trains at a station. Those affected by Dyspraxia and ME may have difficulties in managing their luggage whilst those with Attention Deficits may easily become distracted by the shops/people etc. in a busy station. Some people may misread/misinterpret the numbers on signs and so arrive at the wrong platform at the wrong time! (This difficulty is likely to be caused by conditions such as Occulomotor Delay, Occulomotor Dyspraxia, Scotopic Sensitivity Irlen Syndrome, Dyslexia and Dyscalculia. Problems in understanding the voice giving instructions over the tannoy system are likely to occur if Central Auditory Processing Disorder or Receptive language difficulties are present. Those affected by Attention Deficits may not focus attention on the right piece of information either visually, or, especially auditorily. Individuals affected by Autistic Spectrum Disorder may be unaware of what is going on around them/become disturbed, distressed when using a different route.

The pleasures of travelling by coach/car/boat/train/elephant!

Those with balance difficulties (Dyspraxia) may be travel sick. This can be very acute e.g. the person may only be able to travel the distance between one stop and another on a bus. Travel sickness may not start until the infant is several months old. Naturally, it starts when one is least prepared for it as many a parent knows to their cost. Some car suspensions reduce the likelihood of being sick so it is always best to take the travel sick person with you when choosing a new car. There is less likelihood of being sick if the individual is travelling in the front seat. If the person is travelling in the back seat then it is best to have a car where the back windows wind down fully as the sickness can sometimes be reduced if the person is able to breathe a lot of fresh air. For the same reason it is best not to put the car heater on. True, this means that everyone in the car has to dress in warm winter clothing and even then they can be cold but it does stop the person throwing up! Sleeping children can be affected by travel sickness too. The authoress has vivid memories of her daughter sleeping throughout the journey and then throwing up as soon as the car stopped! Sickness is less likely on a train than in a car/coach but the back seats of coaches are best avoided. Travel sickness can occur on swings, roundabout rides and yes (as the authoress knows only too well) one can also be travel sick on an elephant!

There are various effective anti-sickness preparations on the market which are available from one's doctor, chemist and homeopath. (Pregnant women should always seek such professional advice as to the suitability of a preparation.). Only a few medicines are suitable for the very young child and some of the liquid ones can make the child become hyperactive for hours on end - not a good experience when one arrives at the destination in the early hours of the morning! Stugeron is one of the better treatments. It does not taste and does not make one sleepy. Travel sickness is distressing for all concerned! (Some children can also be distressed when the headlights of oncoming traffic dip in and out of their vehicle when they are travelling on the roads at night.)

Chapter 10
LEISURE
Section 1: Passive forms of leisure

TV/video & cinema

Those affected by Attention Deficits, Autistic Spectrum Disorder and some forms of Occulomotor Dyspraxia may be glued to the television. Those affected by Autistic Spectrum Disorder may prefer to watch a video and will rewind and watch the same bit endlessly. Those affected by Attention Deficits may  be precocious. Children affected by this condition may watch programmes more suitable for an older age group. As this group can become television addicts it may be wise to only have educational games on the home computer and not let them have a television in their bedroom. This love of television can be useful as such children (who may well be reluctant readers) can learn a lot of information if encouraged to watch wild life programmes and documentaries etc.. Some of those affected by this condition cannot settle to watch TV or sit through a whole film at the cinema (or let anybody else do so in peace either!). With certain forms of Occulomotor Dyspraxia there may be less strain on the eyes when watching the television.

Reading

(Conditions: Dyslexia, Attention Deficits, Occulomotor Delay, Occulomotor Dyspraxia, Scotopic Sensitivity Irlen Syndrome)

 People in this group may prefer/need to use audio tapes, computers and/or /hand held Dictionaries whenever possible. Some libraries will allow children with these conditions to borrow audio tapes of stories as a free service. (The age at which the person has to start paying for the tapes seems to vary from county to county.)

Audio tapes can be an ideal form of entertainment on long car journeys especially for those who become travel sick if they try to read when travelling.

Board games

Games can be used to improve sub-skills which are needed for literacy, numeracy and language development. However, games that could help are often avoided by the person for a variety of reasons. Some may fear or dislike letters/numbers and have difficulties in playing the games because of weak spatial and visualisation skills. Those with language difficulties may find even the simplest of language games stressful due to problems such as 'word-finding' difficulties where they cannot access from their mind the word that they want. Such students as well as those affected by Dyspraxia can have difficulties in correctly interpreting and using the rules of the game. Reading the rules of the game may not help here especially if the person also has weak reading/comprehension skills. Individuals with any of these difficulties will need plenty of support from friends and relatives and need to be able to win the first few games. (As the authoress remembers only too well from her childhood playing a game that you always lose is no fun at all.) Those affected by Autistic Spectrum Disorder are unlikely to play board games with other people but will watch the play and may touch/sniff/lick etc. the board and its pieces. (They may also mimic the actions of the players.)

Number games

Those affected by Dyscalculia tend to avoid games with numbers e.g. dominoes. The game of Rummikub (which is part of the Next Generation's 'Take of with Number' Pack) can help improve numeracy skills and reduce the person's fear/dislike of numbers.

Word games

Those affected by Dyslexia may avoid games with words/letters e.g. Scrabble. Scrabble can be made more pleasurable for this group if they are encouraged to use a Franklins handheld spellchecker with a wordbuilder facility in it. The person then just

enters their letters into the spellchecker which then shows
them all the words that they can make. The player still has
to use skill to work out where best to play those letters.

Visualisation and spatial games
Those whose spatial skills are weak (as can be found in
Dyspraxia and Dyscalculia) may avoid (or be poor at)
games where spatial skills are needed e.g. Connect 4,
chess and Othello. Skills can be improved in these areas by playing
Connect 4. In order to be effective it does have to be
introduced in a particular way - see Next Generation's 'Hints on
Using Connect 4/Spatial skills booklets.

Visualisation is the ability to see 'in one's mind' what something
will look like. This skill is necessary when planning future moves
in any of the above strategy games. Those with a weakness in this
area are likely to avoid (frequently lose) such games. 'Battleships'
can be difficult for these students whilst those affected by Attention
Deficits may find this game boring as they may not get a reward
for action quick enough. This can be overcome by increasing the
number of ships on the board so that there will be more 'hits'.

Language games
Playing 'I spy' can be difficult for those affected by language
difficulties but he board game version of it (called 'I-spy' produced
by Living and Learning) makes the game much more fun. 'Guess
Who' (usually available from Argos) is another good game and for
those with wordfinding difficulties the 'Guess my Name Game' by
Ravensburger is particularly useful.

Poor co-ordination skills

(Dyspraxia)
People with these difficulties may avoid any games that involve
balancing, skipping, kicking/catching balls etc. Many of these
games are played in the street/playground and provide not only
opportunities for exercise but for social interaction too. Students
with these difficulties may not be invited into games of tag if they
have problems in knowing when they have been touched or have

difficulties in understanding the rules as can occur with Dyspraxia. The board game Twister can help improve co-ordination. It can also reduce left/right confusion if the instructions for each movement are given carefully. If the student needs hints as to which is left and right it is best to only give him/her something to remember one of them by. Thus no matter which limb the child has the move the parent tells the child the way of remembering his/her left arm e.g. the one with the watch on. So, if the child has to move his right arm he knows that the one with the watch on is his left arm and that his right arm is the 'other one'.

Sport

Those affected by Dyspraxia may have great problems with many sports. Those affected by Dyslexia may find following a sequence in sports such as aerobics confusing and knowing which goal to aim for on a football pitch difficult.

Roller blading can be difficult for those affected by Dyspraxia because of the balance and co-ordination of movements that is required. However, if started young (and given plenty of support) those with moderate to mild difficulties may be able to progress and enjoy this sport.

Swimming - the presence of Dyspraxia will make the co-ordination of strokes (and then combining strokes with the correct breathing) complex. Swimming lessons can cause problems for several reasons. Those affected by Central Auditory Processing Disorder may find it difficult to understand the teacher's instructions because the pool's acoustics distort the teacher's voice. The person affected by Attention Deficits may find all the noise and bustle too distracting to be able to concentrate on learning to swim.

Games involving dynamic perception

This difficulty is found as part of Dyspraxia. It causes difficulties with any ball and bat/ball game. Some people have to concentrate so hard that they may only be able to predict the movement of the shuttlecock/ball for about fifteen to twenty minutes of a game. The rest of the game is spent feeling a complete idiot as they only work out its likely position just as it lands!

Hockey
This seems easier than most as it is virtually a 2D game rather than a 3D one as the ball is always close to the ground.

Volley ball
This is not likely to be a very good game for those affected by Dyspraxia as one needs considerable strength in the forearm to achieve some of the shots. The continuous changing of starting position can make it very confusing for those with sequencing difficulties (Attention Deficits and Dyslexia) and impossible to get 'one's eye in' for working out ball trajectories.

Badminton doubles
This can be quite good as one can play front or back if the partner agree. This enables the player to only have to predict across a narrower range of shuttlecock trajectories and therefore makes it easier to return the shuttlecock. It has an advantage over tennis in that the racket is much lighter and the shuttlecock takes much less effort to move than the tennis ball. There is also the advantage of a playing in a smaller court so there is less far to move when you eventually work out where the shuttlecock is likely to go.

Aerobics/keep fit
This may well not be the ideal sport for those affected by any of the conditions found within the Specific Learning Difficulties Profile. If there are sequencing and/or memory difficulties the person could still be going in one direction whilst the rest of the class are going in another. (Water aerobics is definitely not any slower than normal aerobics and there are the poor acoustics to cope with when trying to listen to the instructions.)

The individual needs to be close to the instructor so that there is a better chance of accurately hearing and seeing/following the actions. However, this does mean that the person needs to be at the front of the hall and so everyone can see when he/she is going wrong. The alternative is to stand right at the back, make all the mistakes you want and feel less of a fool. There is also the added advantage that no-one is likely to run into you when you are going in the wrong direction!

Martial arts
These can be helpful in raising people's self esteem and give them confidence though one does have to be careful that the reckless person affected by Attention Deficits does understand and abide by the rules of contests. There are a variety of martial arts to choose from and it really is a case of looking around. The more gentle ones are Judo and Aikido

Medau
This is a lovely graceful form of movement class where (to a certain extent) you can do your own thing. Unfortunately, classes seem to be few and far between.

Walking
Fresh air and exercise are important for us all and perhaps they are even more important for those affected by Dyspraxia who need to work at keeping their body supple. It is important to wear shoes that cushion the feet as there can be a tendency to exert a lot of downward pressure when walking. Gentle walking can be relaxing and does not put too much stress on the body. Walking a dog is even better and more relaxing.

Yoga
This is good for relaxation and for keeping the body stretched and supple. There are many different forms of it, some concentrate on lots of movements whilst others concentrate on the relaxation side.

Play parks
It is important that young children gain plenty of regular experience in play parks. This will help to improve physical skills

if they are delayed/weak and relieve some of the stress of trying to cope with daily life. Children with Attention Deficit Hyperactivity Disorder can benefit from daily trips to the park to let off some of their excess energy.

The Arts (this includes museums, art galleries etc)

Painting

Those with poor spatial skills (Dyspraxia) and perception skills may find art frustrating. Fine motor difficulties can result in poor control of the brush. The good quality art software that is around now enables students to produce really pleasing artwork but the programs are memory hungry and so the household computer may need upgrading.

Clay

Those affected by Dyspraxia or Autistic Spectrum Disorder may either hate or love touching clay whilst for others it can be very relaxing to mould. If co-ordination problems are present it may be easier to produce slab pottery (from flat slabs of clay) than coil pots (sausages of clay wound round and round) or using a potter's wheel.

Music (Also see inside back cover of this book)

All those affected by the Specific Learning Difficulty Profile can benefit from learning music. It can be a very good outlet for reducing stress and working through one's emotions. It improves the student's ability to understand, discriminate, sequence and process auditory information. It also improves co-ordination and rhythm. Singing and playing a musical instrument also speeds up the corpus callosum part of the brain that is used to send messages from one side of the brain to the other. Music should be started as young as possible (some group classes are available for toddlers – ask at your library for details.) Once started the tuition should be kept going though there may need to be a change of instrument/ type of class along the way!

It is important to choose the instrument carefully - it is only to easy to choose one on the basis of its good looks or sound and not realise that it will be too difficult for a particular student to play. If the chosen instrument does prove to be problematical the student will need a great deal of support and encouragement if he/she is to succeed in playing it. Both the parents and student must then be prepared for it to take a long time to learn. Difficulties in crossing the midline (an imaginary vertical line going down the centre of the body) are commonly found with Dyspraxia. This can cause problems with learning such instruments as the violin and cello. The creation of an embouchure (a particular movement of the lips) is necessary to play the flute and this could be a problem for those with Articulatory Dyspraxia. The weak shoulder girdle that can be part of Dyspraxia makes learning the flute, and the violin difficult

Good spatial skills are needed to play an instrument like the trombone where it is the position of the slide which determines the note. Players of percussion instruments such as drums need to be able to keep the beat for everyone else which requires a very good sense of rhythm. This can cause problems for those affected by Dyslexia and Dyspraxia.

Apparently the tin whistle is the easiest instrument to learn and the recorder is also fairly easy too. Reading music can be a problem for those with Occulomotor Dyspraxia and those who have difficulties in remembering symbols. Colour coded music books for recorder are available from good music shops.

It is easier to learn the keyboard than the piano (as it does not have a foot pedal). There is also only one stave of music to look at. The student can be taught the hand movements as for a piano (rather than just using the one finger chord facility available on the keyboard) so that he/she can transfer to a piano later if desired.

Fortunately, all of us can appreciate music, attend concerts and listen to music at home.

Chapter 11
SKILLS NEEDED FOR THE WORKPLACE

Various skills are needed for the workplace of which many have already been covered in earlier chapters of this book e.g. social skills, memory etc.. *(Further information on the skills mentioned below can be found in the various literacy guides published by Next Generation.)*

Writing

Writing can be made more difficult and stressful if an unsuitable pen, paper and penhold are used. The student should try out pens to find the one that suits him/her best - this service is available at old fashioned stationers. A suitable pen is one that the student finds easy to hold and that glides across the paper with the minimum of pressure. The pen that is ideal for one person is not the pen that will be ideal for another.

Paper should be smooth and of good quality as the pen will then meet little resistance and it will take less energy and pressure to make it move. Recycled paper tends to be less smooth. Often it is the case that the more expensive papers are better to write on but the student needs to avoid choosing papers which have uneven surfaces.

Computers

Many of those affected by the Specific Learning Difficulties Profile would be lost without their computers. Unfortunately, there are still too many schools and college departments with antiquated computers which run software that is word led rather than icon led. This software is not suitable for those with Dyslexia. They do not have suitable spellcheckers in them and are not easy to use.

 Modern computers can run programs like Word 7 (available for Windows '95 machines) which has a good spelling and grammar checker and is easy to use. Being able to use a modern PC is fast becoming an essential life skill both for the

workplace and for the home. Many of those affected by the Profile take to modern computers like 'a duck to water'. Some of those affected by Dyspraxia can be reluctant to use them and prefer to write even if they find handwriting difficult. Dictation programs are now widely available at remarkably cheap prices compared with just a couple of years ago. They all require training and may not be suitable for the young teenage boy when his voice breaks. There have been rapid advances in this technology recently which have considerably reduced the price of such programs. Older programs required the dictator to speak with a pause between every word which can be very irritating and frustrating. The newer programs enable the speaker to use a more normal dictation style without such pauses. If the person is prepared to put in the time to train the program dictation software can be a very worthwhile investment. Up-to-date information on these programs is available from Becta *(see page 67)*.

Hand held spellcheckers: Franklins is still the recommended one but the design of keys on some of the more recent models may not suit everyone as there is no distinct feel of the key going down when you press it. Their products range from discreet and moderately priced credit card size ones to a much larger talking one. The latter has several worthwhile facilities including a phonological guide to every word but the price may be beyond many people's pockets.

Fire drills: All of those who are affected by Autistic Spectrum Disorder may have great difficulties in entering and leaving a building via a different route. They like those with hyperacusis and Central Auditory Processing Disorder can also find the sound of the fire alarm distressing

'Memory Cards' -A way to avoid embarrassment/difficult situations – Slip the appropriate small cards into the wallet/purse/ pencil case of individuals. The set contains the basic information needed for many literacy/numeracy based tasks. It includes spellings of numbers when writing a cheque, mathematical facts (e.g. times tables, geometry, units of measurement, how to do different types of sums), punctuation, sentence starts, confusable words, adding endings to words, spellings, grammar etc.. *(Available from 'Memory Cards, 21 Princes Avenue, Carshalton, Surrey SM5 4NZ)*

Chapter 12
CHOOSING A PET

The presence of the Specific Learning Difficulty Profile within the family can have an affect on the sort of animal chosen for a pet.

It is best to start with the easy pets first. Goldfish and budgies come into this group. They require very little maintenance, and do not take up much room. They have the added advantage that other people may not mind caring for them whilst the family is away on holiday.

Small animals such as cats, rabbits, hamsters, gerbils etc. require little care but they do bite. Those with an over sensitivity to smell may dislike caring for rabbits.

 It is essential that children learn to hold/handle a pet without causing it distress or harm. The child who is affected by Dyspraxia may need to be shown repeatedly how to do this. Some individuals have a tendency not to cuddle the animal but to hold it (without enough support) at a distance from their body. The child with Attention Deficits may detest the pet one minute and be all over it the next and can expect the pet to arrive fully trained! Sometimes, the introduction of a pet can help children with low self-esteem as they have something that loves them and never tells them off, nags them etc.. However, some cats, rabbits etc. do not like being handled and will not conveniently curl up on the child's lap. (The worse thing that can happen is that it curls up on someone else's lap and the child's self esteem plummets again!)

Dogs need a lot of training. Individuals with Attention Deficits may resent the amount of attention the pet needs in order for the training to occur. They may also act impulsively with the pet and not think of the end result of their actions. It may be fun to let the puppy try to catch your shoelaces one day but it is a disaster when they chew them off and never leave your feet alone. Once the dog learns that such behaviour is fun (e.g. he enjoys the screaming, and chasing the violent moving foot) it can be VERY difficult to get him out of the habit. It is best to get a non-dominant puppy e.g. do not pick the one that walks boldly towards you when you go to look at them. If the family is under a lot of stress then choose a breed that does not need a lot of attention (e.g. grooming) and exercise. Surprisingly, some of the larger dogs need comparatively little exercise whilst some of the little ones are the exact opposite. Local dog clubs can provide plenty of information on the different breeds of dogs (their details will be available at your local vet/library).

Those affected by Autistic Spectrum Disorder or Dyspraxia may find it difficult to adjust to the changes a dog brings to the household. The child with Autistic Spectrum Disorder may handle the dog inappropriately e.g. try to smell it or never let it go. Self esteem can improve if the child learns to control the pet but if it is wanted for that reason get one that is very easy to train and choose a breed that likes children!

Before getting the pet it is best to visit other families with the same sort of pet (or your local dog club) to see how your child reacts to and handles it. It is also wise to decide beforehand who will clear up after it, feed it etc. and discuss the changes that the pet will bring into the household.

The introduction of a cat or a dog may create too much stress for a family already overstretched because of the presence of the Specific Learning Difficulty Profile. Alternatively, it may be the solution to each member of the family having something that gives its love unconditionally.

Chapter 13
HOUSEWORK

Those affected by Dyspraxia can have difficulties in moving/ controlling the vacuum cleaner and may knock things over when dusting. Housework can be very tiring for such individuals. Any task which involves raising the arms to shoulder height and above e.g. spring cleaning the top of the kitchen cupboards, washing windows, putting out the washing can be painful if a weak shoulder girdle is present.

Cleaning the stairs can be particularly difficult if there is little muscle strength and/or balancing difficulties as one has to balance both one's own body, the cleaning appliance plus use the appliance in the cleaning process. It is obviously best to have a vacuum cleaner that will fit nicely onto the stair tread to make the task easier. An alternative is to use a small hand-held vacuum cleaner to clean the stairs. If asthma is present in the family vacuum cleaners with special filters can be bought that remove many of the allergens/dust mites out of the environment.

As the upstairs of a house is usually less dirty than the downstairs a lightweight carpet cleaner could be kept upstairs for general cleaning tasks. The vacuum cleaner would then only have to be taken upstairs once a month.

If knocking things over when dusting is a problem then reducing the number of ornaments on display at any one time will help. If associated body movements are just causing the dust to fly around rather than be removed then damp dusting may be easier to achieve than dusting with a dry duster .

Both those affected by Dyspraxia and those affected by Autistic Spectrum Disorder may be very rigid in the way that housework is tackled. For some of this group everything has to be done in a particular way and/or order e.g. when hanging out the washing the pegs must always be in one particular position on each type of garment.

Washing-up by hand is not only a tiresome task but also (in the hands of someone affected by Dyspraxia) a very wet one. The water can pour over the edges of the sink unit, down one's clothes and puddle at one's feet. In an ideal world one would use a dishwasher - the saving grace of many of us. However, the world is not  ideal and all of us from time-to-time will still need to wash some things by hand. A sink unit that has a stainless steel top with a lip all the way round it can keep some of the water in. A rolled up towel laid across the front of the unit acts as a dam to catch most of the water. A large washing up bowl is easier to use than a small one as the hand movements do not need to be so cramped. For once luck is on our side as it is actually more hygienic to leave the items to drain than to use a tea towel to dry them

It is sometimes easier to wash the kitchen floor using a cloth and bucket rather than trying to control an unwieldy mop. Of course, one could just choose a kitchen flooring that does not show the dirt too much. The ultimate solution is to pay someone else to do the housework! Some people are particularly rigid in the way that they  want things done or have low self-esteem/ fear what the cleaner will think of the state of the house. This group may actually clean a lot of the house before the cleaner arrives so defeating the object of the exercise!

A parent is likely to have to supervise a child affected by Attention Deficits or Autistic Spectrum Disorder when they are using household cleaning agents (and depending upon the severity of the condition this supervision may have to continue into adulthood). The former child may impulsively spray the container in someone's eyes whilst the latter may try to drink, smell or touch it. Some spray containers are quite fiddly to use for those affected by Dyspraxia. Cleaning sinks is made easier (and little or no scrubbing is involved) if one pours a solution of bleach

into it and leaves it for ten to fifteen minutes. However, this might not be such a wise thing to do if one has an impulsive child who may decide to drink it, play with it etc..

Possibly the best advice to give to someone who finds housework stressful, tiring, (or perhaps in the case of those affected by Attention Deficits - just plain boring) is to do as much as you feel happy doing. If anyone else in the family is not happy with that solution then they are the ones who can do it!!!

The family which has one or more members affected by the Specific Learning Difficulty Profile is automatically under more stress than other families. Those parents affected by Dyspraxia and Autistic Spectrum Disorder may only be able to cope with life if their house is tidy and very clean. This can put an even greater strain on the family but it is often difficult (if not impossible) for such people to change. In reality it is more important for the family to socialise and relax together than it is to have a clean and tidy house. So, the ultimate solution may be (on at least some days of the week) to ignore the housework and go away from the house as then the dirt and mess etc. cannot be seen!

Dyspraxia Foundation 8 West Alley, Hitchin, Herts SG5 1EG
Tel: 01462 454986
Adult Helpline: 01714355443

AFASIC - overcoming Speech Impairments (Only *deals with children.)* 347 Central Markets, Smithfield, London EC1A 9NH
Tel: 0171 2363632

The ADHD Family Support Group UK c/o Mrs G Mead, 1A High St, Dilton Marsh, Westbury, Wiltshire BA13 4DL Tel: 01373 826045

The National Autistic Society 393 City Road, London EC1V 1NE
Tel: 0171 833 2299

The British Dyslexia Association 98 London Road, Reading, RG1 5AU.
Helpline: 0118 966 8271

Scottish Dyslexia Association Unit 3, Stirling Business Centre, Wellgreen Place, Stirling, Scotland FK8 2DZ Tel: 01786 446650

Adult Dyslexia Association 336 Brixton Road, London SW9 7AA   Tel: 0171 924 9559

Action for ME PO Box 1302, Wells, Somerset BA5 1YE   Tel: 01749 670799

USEFUL BOOKS
You mean I'm not lazy, stupid or crazy? by Kate Kelly & Peggy Ramundo. Lots of practical advice for adults affected by Attention Deficits ISBN 0 684 80116 7

Perceptuo-Motor Difficulties by Dorothy Penso. Practical advice on overcoming the difficulties caused by dyspraxia. ISBN 0 412 39810 9

The Autistic Spectrum by Lorna Wing. Practical advice for parents & professionals.
ISBN 0 09 475160 9

Get Ahead by North & Buzan. Teaches Mind Mapping
ISBN 1 874374 00 7

RELATIONSHIPS SERVICES IN THE UK
Relate: provides a marriage/ partnership guidance service
National Family Mediation Service: provides a family mediation in divorce/separation service.
Local information on the availability of the above can be found in your library/telephone directory.

The Relate Guides
(These guides were written by Sarah Litvinoff in co-operation with Relate counsellors and officers of the Relate organisation.)

The relate guide to better relationships Practical ways to make your relationship last.
ISBN 0-09-177432-2

The relate guide to starting again. Learn from past relationships how to build stronger ones in the future.
ISBN 0-09-175295-7.